The 80/20 Blueprint

The concise guide to
working less and
achieving more.

by Stuart Carter

www.stuartcarter.co.uk

I am deeply grateful to those without whom this book would still be just an idea somewhere in my head.

Most notably...

Mohammed Bhojani *who is somehow always ahead of me in identifying my potential.*

Jana Schuberth *who helped me realise I could take the leap.*

My amazing Masterminders *who keep me inspired, clear and accountable.*

...and not forgetting Helen, *my wonderful wife who has supported me—occasionally willingly—through the ups and downs of my sometimes-terrifying business journey!*

—

Thank-you all.

—

Disclaimer

The contents of this book do not constitute individual advice to the reader. The ideas, procedures and suggestions contained in this book are not intended as a substitute for consulting with a professional business adviser. Neither the author nor the publisher shall be held liable or responsible for any loss or damage allegedly arising from any information or suggestion in this book.

THE 80/20 BLUEPRINT

Foreword

by Marc Wileman
founder of Sublime Science

To me 80/20 is not really about "maths", "statistics" or "data-crunching ", it's about something so much more important... *YOUR freedom.*

If you're an entrepreneur or business owner and want to make an impact on this world then chances are there are always a million-and-one things to do.

And the bad news is, there always will be!

This leads to anxiety and stress that can overwhelm all aspects of your life but even worse it can destroy your dreams.

Let's be clear. There's no magic bullet here. No 'easy button'. No magic 'think the special thought and become a millionaire'. But there *is* a deep understanding of how you can practically understand and implement 80/20 into your business and life and quickly see real, solid results.

This is *not* theory. I've personally worked on applying these principles every day for seven years and in that time I've developed a national company, won many high-profile awards, published two books and more importantly made science awesome for 380,000 children through my company *Sublime Science*.

—

There's a pretty uncomfortable truth that goes against everything we're told at school and growing up. Most things don't matter much. But just a few things make a massive amount of difference. I'd go so far as to say that making your dream a reality mandates figuring out which critical few things make most difference and working on them.

Simple but *not* easy.

With that in mind, what Stuart has put together here is a simple, straightforward, actionable system of how to best apply 80/20 into your business and life.

We all want to get more results in less time and Stuart has created a blueprint here that will allow you to do just that.

Dive in, enjoy.

To your success,

'Mad' Marc Wileman
Founder, Sublime Science
www.sublimescience.com

Contents

The 80/20 Blueprint

Read This First

"Don't tell me about your effort.
Show me your results."
— Tim Fargo

Congratulations! You are now holding in your hands a unique book. It's unique because you're only going to read about 20% of it.

First, read the ten business problems on the following pages. Pick out the two that are having the biggest impact on your business right now, and put a star by them... then read on...

10 Business Problems

1. You don't know what's going on in your business, don't know what to measure, or you're overwhelmed by all those "stupid numbers."

2. You're fed up of people whinging and moaning around you, putting down your great ideas, or you feel you're being held back in some way but can't really identify why.

3. You're either not doing any marketing, or you're spending too much with little results to show for it. Or you don't know what's worth spending on.

4. You're bogged down by work that's not completely fulfilling or you feel uneasy in some way doing the work you do. Maybe you haven't found your purpose yet, or suspect you might not be on the right path for fulfillment.

5. You're picking up clients who, quite frankly, are a bit of a pain in the rear to work with. They

want the moon on a stick, then ask for a discount, and then pay late!

6. You don't have time to do everything you need to do in your business, or things you *want* to do in your life.

7. You're overwhelmed by problems in your business. Your to-do list gets longer every day. Or you have problems that seem to have no solution.

8. You're overwhelmed keeping track of products, services, campaigns, customers... juggling too many balls, or spinning too many plates.

9. You're working hard and are pretty successful and comfortable, but not getting the income you'd like to fulfil your dreams.

10. You struggle to get your emails or letters read. People don't respond to your quotes, invoices and other communications.

Good Job!

You've already implemented your first 80/20 action. By picking the two problems that are having the biggest impact on your business and your happiness right now, you've effectively shortened this book by 80%.

You've picked the problems that, if you could solve them, would give you more meaning, more time to do the things you want to do and more freedom to choose how you live your life.

Now all you have to do is read the two chapters relating to the problems you've starred (clue: the numbers match!), and act on them. Then when you're done and you've seen the results, you'll be ready to start living the 80/20 life.

At that point, go and read the chapter, that brings it all together: "The Common Thread".

If you have never been introduced to the 80/20 principle, the following chapter gives a very brief summary. If you *have* been introduced, then please feel free to skip it.

How Not To Fail

Plenty of people read a book, set it aside and fail to act on what they're read.

So here's my challenge to you... take the time you would have spent reading the whole book, and put your effort into reading just two chapters, but *taking rapid and decisive action on what you learn.*

"To know and not to do is really not to know."
— Stephen R. Covey

And if you think you know all about everything written here, then try a slightly different angle. Pick two chapters and gain a *deeper understanding* of what you already know. ***And act this time!***

How To Help Yourself

It's so tempting, when reading about business, to think "yes, very good, that's nice" and then fail to take action. There are a few reasons we fail to act...

1. No-one is holding us accountable
2. It isn't an 'urgent' task
3. We fear getting out of our comfort zone
4. We try to do everything perfectly and do nothing

To help yourself actually achieve these tasks, I suggest you get together with one or more other business owners who are interested in growing *their* business.

Commit and Share

Commit to taking actions based on what you read here. Share your commitments with your group, set deadlines to get the stuff done, and support each other when things get tough. Other people are usually much better at seeing your potential than you are. They don't have the same emotional blocks to your success (though they may have blocks to their own success that you can help with).

The Fallacy of Failure

There will come times when you 'fail' in the classic sense of the word. Failure just means that things didn't go how you hoped they would.

The best way to come to terms with fear of failure is to ask "what have I learnt, and what might I be able to do differently?"

By reframing 'failure' to 'learning' it becomes much easier to act. You end up with a 'win-win' on any task you attempt... the only possible outcomes are that you succeed, or you learn.

You may, in fact, find yourself disappointed when things go exactly your way because you have no opportunity to do it better next time!

On Perfection

The worst thing you can do for your productivity is wait until everything is perfect before letting it out there in the big wide world.

It will *never* be perfect. It will *never* be ready.

So get it good enough and get it out there. Something that's 93% finished is as effective as something that's 0% finished if it's not out there bringing value to the world.

You can always revise it later.

Go!

So... set some time aside, switch off your phone, close your email and get on to your two chapters.

And rock it!

80/20 in a Nutshell

Not All Effort Is Equal

If you have not yet been introduced to the 80/20 principle (or Pareto Principle), let me summarise very quickly here.

The 80/20 principle was first noted in 1896 by Italian economist Vilfredo Pareto. Pareto noticed that 80% of the land in Italy was owned by 20% of the population.

He then went on to discover that 80% of the peas in his garden were in 20% of the pods.

Further study of the principle over the years, and popularisation by Richard Koch, Perry Marshall and Tim Ferriss (see *further reading*) have shown that the principle holds true for many, many phenomena in nature and in business.

Almost anything that can be measured shows the principle to a greater or lesser extent.

It may not be exactly 80/20... it could be 70/20 or 90/10 or 50/20... but the common theme is that all inputs are not equal when it comes to the resulting outputs.

Or to put it another way, not all effort is rewarded the same amount. Some effort is valuable. Other effort is not so valuable. And taken to further extremes some effort is *extremely* valuable. And some is just wasting your time and energy.

How To Use 80/20

The 80/20 principle encourages us to find and exploit situations where effort is rewarded well. To put our resources into the most effective aspects of our life and business, instead of wasting time, money and energy on less effective work.

Throughout this book, you'll find practical examples, applying the principle to day-to-day problems.

And once you've become aware, see where you can spot this imabalance of effort-to-reward in your daily life.

Being habitually aware of the 80/20 principle is a little like *The Matrix;* when the veil is lifted and you suddenly begin to see life how it really is instead of how you've always seen it before.

The 80/20 Blueprint

1. Measuring Your Business

> "If a measurement matters at all, it is
> because it must have some conceivable
> effect on decisions and behaviour. If we
> can't identify a decision that could be
> affected by a proposed measurement and
> how it could change those decisions, then
> the measurement simply has no value"
> — Douglas W. Hubbard

Know your numbers

John loves to measure. He runs a consultancy
business and measures his revenue, outgoings,
overheads, number of clients, fuel consumption,

time usage and a whole host of other things in his business.

He has learnt that to succeed you must "know your numbers" and religiously updates his spreadsheets every day. Before he measured everything he was winging it at best; never sure if his business would survive into the next month. Measuring gives him an enormous sense of well-being.

But John has a new problem. All this measurement is overwhelming. He has twenty different numbers he knows he needs to improve, and just the chore of updating them all makes him wonder if it's even worth being in business in the first place.

Let's look at John's situation, and apply some smart 80/20 thinking to it...

Not all measurements are the same

Hubbard's quote at the start of this chapter says it all. What are you measuring in your business? If you're not going to take action on it, don't bother measuring it!

Not all measurements in business are the same. And not all businesses have the same set of important measurements. So have a look at your business now, and check what you're measuring. You'll fall into one of three camps:

1. Blindness

The 'blind' approach has one of two problems... either you measure nothing and therefore have no idea what's going on; or you measure things and fail to look at—or act on—the measurements. Both are as dangerous, though the latter carries the added penalty of wasted time!

2. Ninja Measurement

You're on it. You're measuring the stuff that matters and acting on it appropriately. Question... why are you reading this chapter? You might review the measurements you're making, to check that what was once relevant still is.

3. Over-measuring

If this is you, you're like John. You're measuring too much stuff in your business. Look at which measurements you're never going to act on and eliminate them. Look at which measurements don't actually give a useful indicator of success. Can you eliminate those too?

Simplify and take action

Once you've simplified your measurements (or decided which small set of measurements you're going to take) make a system of reviewing and acting on them.

Do you have a default diary in your business or do you wing it, reacting to emails and phone calls that come in?

Each month, each week or each day you should be able to say which of your measurements you're actively working on improving.

Do you have targets for each of your measurements? If not, how do you know when you're succeeding?

The power of compounding

And remember that a 10% increase in just four distinct measurements could lead to a 46% growth in your business due to the amazing power of compounding.

Once you've dealt with the big stuff, you might want to surf the 'slight edge' and improve lots of little things by 1% each. But until everything's already pretty successful, focus on the big wins; those 10% and 20% improvements that can be made by smartly measuring the right stuff, and acting on it!

The 20%...

Don't be tempted to measure too much in your business. Only measure:

1) Things that are going to make a significant impact.

2) Things that you are actually going to act on.

Make a system for acting on and improving the measurements you're making.

2. Hanging Around with the Right People

> "You are the average of the five
> people you spend most time with."
> — Jim Rohn

Make a list, right now, of the five people you spend the most time with. Now go through the list and figure if they're going to help you get to your goals, or hold you back.

Usually with any group of five, there will be one really good influence. Someone who supports you and has your back whatever you decide to do. And there will usually be one pretty bad influence. Someone who puts down your ideas, or plants negative seeds in your mind, or holds you back through small-mindedness or envy.

The other three in your group may be more 'neutral', but will still show tendancies towards the positive or the negative – towards helping you or hindering you with your goals.

Most people are generally "red-lighters" or "green-lighters" and once you start seeing more clearly, you'll begin to spot them easily. The table opposite shows some characteristics to look out for...

Be Aware

The 80/20 approach to relationships is to constantly be aware of who are the right people to be hanging around with, and make sure you spend as much time with them as possible.

Use whatever excuses you need; go to seminars, go for coffee or beers or lunch. Or one of the most

Red-Lighters	Green-Lighters
Talk about scarcity (not enough money/ work to go around)	Talk about abundance (there is plenty of everything!)
Talk about other people or the past.	Talk about ideas.
Value security.	Value freedom.
Compete.	Collaborate.
See problems and obstacles.	See solutions and opportunities.
Exhibit fear.	Exhibit hope and faith.
Blame others.	Take Responsibility.

Table 1. Tell-tale characteristics of Red-Lighters and Green-Lighters.

powerful ways you can hang around with the right people is to build a Master Mind group.

Master Mind

Out of everyone you know, there will be a key group who really understand you and your business. They wholeheartedly support your vision; even if it's not their idea of a vision; not how *they* would bring success to *their* life.

Bringing these people together in a Master Mind group is the best way to ensure you keep generating new ideas, supporting each other and sharing honest feedback and that all-important accountability around the table.

By way of example, the Master Mind group I'm in meets for five hours every month—a huge investment—and is in daily contact through a private facebook group. Each day we say what we've done "I have..." and what we'll do tomorrow "I will..."

In fact, this book would not be in your hands if my Master Minders hadn't devised a pretty bad penalty for me if the draft wasn't ready in time for the next meeting.

Since the book is in your hands, you can sleep easy, safe in the knowledge that I still don't know what Chappie dog food tastes like!

More on Red-Lighters

If you have "red-lighters" in your sphere of influence, whether that's your friends, a business group, or in your facebook newsfeed, you really need to do what you can to reduce exposure.

That doesn't mean being rude, or being mean to anyone. It just means doing what you need to do if you're going to hit your goals.

"Unfollow" is your friend on facebook... you don't have to stop being friends, but you can prevent the negativity of these red-lighters from rubbing off on you on a daily basis.

Family and Old Friends

You may be in the difficult situation where your family or old friends or spouse are red-lighters. And I'm not saying you should disown them. But you may need to limit the amount of your vision and business you share with them.

Old friends and family can keep you grounded, to keep your vision on track with your true values so some exposure is vital. But as you become more successful, the person you become will be vastly different from the person they're "used to".

Expectations

Our loved ones can have a completely different mindset to us, and can put expectation on you to conform to the script they've written for you. So while we may love them and value them greatly, sharing the risks of business can backfire badly.

T. Harv Ecker's book "*Secrets Of The Millionaire Mind*" and Gay Hendricks' "*The Big Leap*" both deal with the problems we face when we out-grow the blueprint we've been given from our upbringing.

What else do you let in?

Everything that applies to the people you're physically hanging around with also applies to your choice of reading and entertainment. Have a look at the last five books you read... do they serve your purpose in life?

Now, you might use fiction books to wind down, and that's fine. If you're using them deliberately that's good. If you find yourself reading stuff that isn't helping you to relax or get ahead, it might be worth revisiting your choices.

The Media

And your choice of news and entertainment... does it enrich your life? Does it inspire you and motivate you? Or does it encourage fear or lethargy?

So many people start their day with the news. They let fear, violence and hatred into their life at the most influential part of the day.

If you're running a social enterprise to deal with fear, violence and hatred I can see the benefit of catching up on world events. Otherwise it's a mere distraction.

Gratitude

I guess the other benefit of catching up on the news is that you can be grateful that none of that bad stuff is happening to you personally.

But you can be grateful without having to see the flip-side. Look around you. Look at what you have, at the bounty of love, opportunity and possibility around you. Be grateful for that.

The 20%...

*Who are you allowing to influence you,
both in real life and through the media and
entertainment?*

*Find the 20% who will help you and your business
grow and spend as much time as possible with
them - with a Master Mind group if possible.*

*Don't necessarily disown the "red-lighters" but do
reduce your exposure.*

3. Marketing Like a Ninja

> *"Before you eat the elephant, make sure you know what parts you want to eat."*
> — Todd Stocker

Meet Rob

Rob is a wedding photographer. He gets loads of enquiries and meets lots of soon-to-be-wed couples. But his conversion rate is very poor.

One of the reasons for this is that Rob is really not the cheapest photographer. His packages start at £5,000, and this really puts off a lot of his potential clients, however much they like him when they meet.

One day Rob made a tiny change to his marketing. He knew that putting price-lists online wasn't very good for his industry... he didn't want to attract people who are shopping on price, he wanted to attract people who value his artistic skill.

But the little change he made was to add ten words to his 'contact' page...

"If you'd like to work together *and have at least £5,000 to invest in your photography,* let's talk..."

By setting the £5,000 minimum, his enquiry rate dropped to a 5th of the previous rate. But his conversion rate soared! In fact, Rob was getting the same number of clients while only meeting 20% of the couples he used to.

All that travelling, spending time in meetings, drinking gallons of tea, preparing quotes, following them up... all saved by a tiny pre-qualifying sentence.

And the time and money he saved on those dead-end leads could now be spent looking after the good ones.

Spend time, money and energy

The key to winning the battle for your potential customers' attention is to spend time, money and energy on them. To engage them, to convey your value and trustability, to bring them great value before ever demanding payment in return. The person who can help most before asking for payment will prevail.

But how do you know who is worth spending that time, money and energy on? You don't want to cast pearls before swine as the proverb goes.

Get Them To Show Themselves

The key is to pre-qualify your prospects. Put small stuff out there that will cause interested parties to identify themselves by responding in some way (or, indeed to get disinterested parties to filter themselves out of the process).

You can do the same with your prospective clients. You want people who won't argue with your prices? Well, how about saying...

"We won't do discounts, but we will do a great job!"

Have a look around you for pre-qualification strategies that others are using. As you become aware, you'll spot them more and more often. Sometimes they're bold and brash, throwing down the gauntlet to their target audience...

"If you like fast food, this restaurant is not for you!"

Trying to please

One of the big dangers in business is trying to be all things to all people. It results in a 'beige' business that doesn't have any true values.

When you stop trying to please everyone, you can let your values shine. Granted you might only get 20% of the enquiries you used to, but like Rob, those enquiries will be from people who really understand you, and appreciate how you work.

The scarcity mindset is scared by the prospect of losing 80% of their enquiries. The abundance mindset realises that those 20% of enquiries will bring true wealth. Those 20% will value the work done and pay handsomely for it. What's more, their friends are highly likely to have similar values.

Before you know it, you have more enquiries than ever; and only from people you love working with.

Outspending Your Competition

Now you've figured the quality of your leads and added up the money they're willing to spend with you, you now know how much you can afford to spend to reach these people.

Your competitiors are still firing their 'scatter-gun', spending money getting their marketing message out to as many people as possible, most of whom will never buy from them.

Be The Sniper

You, on the other hand, are now a 'sniper'. You pick out the people who are most likely to re-spond and buy from you and focus your resources directly on them.

Imagine being able to spend £1,000 to get a single client on board. How much goodwill and 'wow-factor' could you generate with £1,000? Once you're not diluting your spend, this kind of thing becomes possible.

The 20%...

Figure out which prospects are most likely to buy from you and value what you do for them. Then instead of spreading your marketing spend wide, focus it on your golden prospects.

You can spend far more per prospect, impress and delight them, and boost your conversions massively.

4. Being a Genius

> "Everybody is a genius. But if you judge a
> fish by its ability to climb a tree, it will live
> its whole life believing that it is stupid."
> — Albert Einstein

Michelle and the New Year Party

Michelle loves parties. And New Year especially!
She loves to have her New Year planned well in
advance, and so when Rachel invited her to her
New Year party in late September she accepted
straight away.

Rachel holds pretty good parties and often invites
plenty of people Michelle knows.

However, in October, Paul invites Michelle to his New Year party. Paul holds absolutely awesome parties... his mates run an events company, so he always gets a PA rig and a really good DJ. He also has a pool at his place... when Paul invites you, you go!

But Michelle is loyal and she's already accepted Rachel's invitation. She loves Rachel as a friend, and would never let her down, but as New Year approaches she has a secret resentment inside.

And on the night of the party, it turns out that a whole bunch of people who would have been at Rachel's have actually gone to Paul's.

It all goes a bit flat.

The Classic Error

In this story, Michelle has made one of the classic errors that hold many people back from being a genius. (Or more accurately—given Einstein's quote above—from *working with their genius that they already have.*)

One of the hardest parts of running an 80/20-aware business, especially when you haven't lived 80/20 for long enough, is accepting the need to turn down good opportunities.

What? That sounds mad!

Turning Down Good Opportunities

The first step of 80/20 awareness is to get rid of the bad stuff. The bottom 10%... those 10% of customers who demand the earth and don't pay for it; those 10% of employees who don't pull their weight; those 10% of items on your to-do list that just hang around in your headspace and won't bring true value to your business.

This extends to the 10% of opportunities that are either going to take too much of your time, or not help people to your best ability, or not pay well enough or any combination of these.

The next step is to turn down the mediocre stuff. The stuff that is ok, but won't really get you to your goals.

But then comes the ninja step... and it's this one that's the hardest to do... it goes against everything you've learnt – particularly if you come from a sparsity mindset (there isn't enough to go around, so I must grab everything I can)

The ninja step is turning down the GOOD stuff, to leave yourself free to pursue the GREAT stuff.

Blowing It

So what happens when you turn down something good and nothing great comes along? Ok, so you blew it. You missed a chance. But look at the opportunity cost... the payoff if the great opportunity came along. Let's say you miss nine times out of ten, but that tenth GREAT opportunity more than makes up for the nine missed ones... it was still well worth doing and you've worked less too!

It doesn't mean there's anything wrong with the good stuff; except that it takes your time, energy and resources that might be better used elsewhere.

The Genius of Skills

Exactly the same problem that applies to opportunities also applies to your skills, and this is where the 'genius' really starts to come out.

One of the biggest mistakes in business and life is to trying to do everything. Spending time on your weakest skills and abilities to try and improve them.

It's a hang-over of the school system where we're encouraged to focus our time and energy on our D-grades at the expense of rocking out our A-grade subjects.

Troublemaker or Genius?

Imagine, for a moment, if a primary student was absolutely rocking it at maths, but struggling with English, geography and history.

They spend years struggling through those subjects, all the while having their maths held back by their year group.

Imagine if, instead, they could drop all their other subjects and get a maths degree by the age of 14. Then they could begin providing valuable service through research projects. They would almost certainly be called a "genius".

But in today's world, they'll be held back by the school system, get exceedingly bored in their maths lessons and probably instead be labelled "troublemaker".

Imagine that. Transformation from "troublemaker" to "genius" just by implementing 80/20 in a smart way.

Screw Your Weaknesses.

It's time, right now, to forget the blueprint you've picked up in school, and do the unthinkable.

You are hereby no longer expected to do everything yourself... I give you permission to ask the 'smart kid' for help with your homework.

You are hereby no longer expected to improve your bad grades... I give you permission to work more on the stuff you enjoy and are good at, and get someone else to take the subjects you're weaker at.

Outsourcing

Why spend two hours using a bad skill when you could outsource the same work to an expert who can produce the same, or better, in 10 minutes? And you can spend those two hours doing what you do best.

Likewise why spend 30 minutes using a *good* skill when you could get someone in your team who could do better in a shorter time?

One of the characteristics of a good 80/20 practitioner is that they always think in terms of collaboration not competition.

Who can I get to do this hard (for me) stuff, so I can focus on the stuff I'm good at?

The To-Don't List

Make a list of all the things you do right now in your business and life that you either don't enjoy, or are not very good at. Now make a plan to outsource or otherwise stop doing each of those things. Figure out just how much time and mental clarity you'll buy to really focus on the stuff you do well.

By the laws of 80/20, the activities you perform in one percent of your day are fifty times more valuable than your average activities. That's your genius at work. It might be a flash of inspiration, or clicking 'send' on an email campaign that makes you tens of thousands of pounds. By spending more time in that genius zone, our success and income grows rapidly.

We *are* all a genius, we just have to clear out the clutter in order to let our genius shine.

The 20%...

What opportunities do you take, and what skills do you use that are good, mediocre or poor?

Make a plan to stop taking those opportunities and outsource those skills so you can focus purely on the stuff that's most rewarding, most valuable to the world and really allows your genius to shine.

5. Getting the Best Customers

> "*Someone out there is looking for exactly what you've got...and will never try and undercut your value or question your worth. Some things in life just can't be bartered over or placed on the sale rack – and your self-worth is at the top of the list.*"
> — Mandy Hale

Painful Customers

We've all had them. Customers who are a complete pain in the rear. They make unreasonable demands of us, expecting us to provide the moon on a stick, and then trying to barter down the price they're paying for it.

There's actually nothing wrong with these customers. For another supplier they might be an ideal client.

The problem is that they're just not for you. And more importantly, *you're not the one for them.*

Sorting and Grading

The number one task for dealing with your customers (and not just the bad ones) is to sort them according to how rewarding they are, how painful they are to work with, and how much they value what you do.

By the laws of 80/20, you will usually find that you have 20% of customers who are an absolute delight to work with. You enjoy providing your service, they pay well and they're the first to sing your praises to others. We'll call these the "A" clients.

Tip: do everything you can to retain A clients. If they say "jump" you not only ask how high, but make a few suggestions of suitable heights, and ask if they'd like to pay a premium for a two-footed jump.

Below the A-grades, and still a valuable group in your stable, you'll get the middle ground, most likely around 60% of your clients. They're ok, but neither overly joyous nor overly painful to work with. We'll call these the "B" clients.

Then the bottom 20% are truly painful to work with. And we're just going to talk about these for a moment.

Low-Grade Clients

It can seem a little mean to talk about "low-grade" clients. But bear in mind we are not saying these are bad people. I'm sure they contribute to life, they are valuable people deserving respect. But—and this is the key point—they do not value what you can do for them, in the way you do it.

So with that in mind, why would we not allow our 'competitiors' to serve these people. Their values may be much more in tune. You are doing your client, your competitor, and yourself a favour by letting them go.

Turn-Around

We can split the bottom 20% into two further grades... half of them may be turned around. Many times I've heard of business owners attempting to 'sack' a client by doubling their prices. It turns out the client did value the service, but because they weren't paying enough, they weren't sufficiently grateful for what was being done for them.

With new expectations set, and a new reward being set for services rendered they can turn into pretty good clients. Just by raising the issue, it becomes a win for both parties.

The clients you suspect may be good for a turn-around would be graded "C", but time-permitting you should get the issue out in the open as soon as feasible. They could easily be upgraded to "B" or even "A".

The "Bullet List"

However, some clients are not even open to turning around. Again, this should be accepted as a natural law. It's nothing personal. Give me 100 clients, and I'll show you 10 who really don't get what I do for them. These are the "D" grades.

These people, if retained, will take more of your time than anyone else. They'll make you question your self-worth. They'll cause anxiety. And the only solution is to let them go as soon as possible.

That doesn't mean being nasty, or letting them down. If you know people who provide the same service as you, but in a different way, a referral can be a perfect triple win.

But you have to get out of the relationship, otherwise it will be toxic to your future success.

Opportunities

Once you've graded your customers, you need to get more of the good ones. It can be un-nerving to 'sack' clients, especially if your cashflow isn't in a massive surplus.

But just look at the opportunities you'll be opening up to gain more A-grade clients if you're not firefighting the Cs and Ds.

Even if you end up with less income, how much peace of mind do you buy for the sake of letting a few Ds go?

Getting More As

Once you have the time and energy freed by 'sacking' your Ds and turning around your Cs, you can focus on getting more A clients.

What do they have in common? Are your current A-grade clients hanging around with other potential As? Can you get an introduction through a referral or affiliate scheme?

One of my favourite bits of feedback I hear from my clients is when they say (with a huge amount of relief and gratitude in their voice), "I'm now only working with people who are a delight to work with".

If you haven't been through this exercise yet, make it a priority. You won't believe how important it is for your happiness and fulfilment until you've taken the plunge.

Imagine that... only working with people who are a delight to work with, on jobs that you love.

The 20%...

Grade your clients, A to D.

Do everything you can for the As, and encourage them to introduce you to their friends.

See if you can turn the Cs around, they could become Bs or even As.

Sack the Ds and buy yourself some peace of mind and energy for finding more As.

6. Creating Time

> "No one can save time. It's not like
> money. You can't deposit the time you
> save into an account and use it later.
> Time passes. Time is a constantly
> depleting resource. Once it's gone, it's
> gone, and you will NEVER get it back."
> — Gudjon Bergmann

The myth of time management

Wouldn't it be amazing if you could create
time? One of the biggest problems I hear from
business owners and, indeed, others is "time
management".

You can't manage time. Time always ticks by whatever you do. But you *can* manage yourself, and create *useful* time. You're going to do it right now.

Let's Create Some Time

When you've finished reading this sentence, just stop, don't try to read on, don't try to do anything, just clear your mind, stare at the wall and count to thirty slowly... ready... go...

Did you do it? If not, go and do it now.

What happened while you were counting? Did you get anxious, thinking you should be doing something with the time? Did you speed up to get it over with? Did it feel like a pretty long time?

Can you think of what tasks you could have performed in that time?

A Little Multplied By A Lot

The problem with time isn't how long things take, or how much of it we have, it's how we use it. Look at how small pieces of wasted time add up to create minutes or hours that could be used more effectively. See how our focus drifts off important tasks, how we think we have to do everything instead of using leverage to get other people doing things; or automating them.

We have 2,880 chunks of 30 seconds in our day. When you counted to thirty on the last page, it felt like a long time, right? We have over two and a half thousand opportunities to use that amount of time to grow our business and ourselves.

And more importantly Richard Branson has those same chunks of time. As does Bill Gates. As does everyone else in the world.

The rules of 80/20 say there are some long tasks you perform; maybe focussing for two hours on a business problem. And there are hundreds of little, tiny, few-second tasks.

Buying Time

You can buy time from the 'tiny task' end to perform more and more 'long tasks'; usually the more valuable ones.

Imagine investing an hour of work to, for example, automate an aspect of your invoicing so you save two minutes every time you write an invoice.

After just thirty invoices you've paid back your investment. Then you have two minutes extra per invoice *for life*.

I did this exercise once in a previous business, and for a thirty minute investment I had saved myself... wait for it... *a week per year.*

That's a week for free, that I could now spend sitting on a beach with my feet up if I so desired, and have exactly the same business I had before.

This stuff is absolutely vital if you're going to grow your business.

The Snowball Effect

The real beauty of these time savings, though, is the compounding effect. I've "bought" a week of time for the price of just thirty minutes. If I now forsake the beach and instead invest that week into buying more time-savings...

Before long I don't have anything to do! Other than, naturally, what I do best. The thing I actually started my business to do in the first place!

Buying Time With Cash

You can also buy time with cash. Let's say you work at an hourly rate of £25 per hour, and do your bookkeeping at the weekend to save money.

You spend, on average, eight hours tearing your hair out over all those silly numbers and receipts and bank statements.

A bookkeeper is experienced and can do the same amount of work in just one hour. And they also charge £25 per hour.

So, for £25 you can buy eight hours of free time to go to the beach with the kids. And you only have to work for one hour in your 'day job' to pay for it.

Does that sound like a good deal?

Will you feel better after your chilled weekend? Will you be more in the mood to go looking for more clients? Will you present a better impression to your prospective customers when they phone you up?

Will you appear more relaxed and confident?

On Deadlines

Have you noticed that when you have a deadline, you get stuff done. It's human nature to expand the time taken over a project to the time allowed.

But do you find that the non-urgent but important stuff gets left until "later" which never comes?

Here's a little hack... if you do the non-urgent stuff first, it ensures it gets done. The urgent stuff has to get done, so even with a shorter time to do it in, you'll find a way!

The 20%...

You can create time by investing in time-saving.

The biggest savings come from small savings multiplied many many times.

You can also buy time for cash.

Deadlines get stuff done, so do the less urgent (but still important) stuff first.

7. Solving Problems

"Happiness is not the absence of problems,
it's the ability to deal with them."
— Steve Maraboli

Dealing with Problems

There are two ways to look at problems in the context of 80/20.

One is "a problem" and the other is "problems". We'll look at "problems" first, as it's the easier to apply 80/20 to.

Multiple Problems

When faced with a multitude of problems, it's pretty clear that it's usually best to focus on the most important ones first; the ones that are having the greatest impact on your endeavours.

But what about quick wins? Are there problems that can be delegated or solved extremely quickly that will have a 'good' impact? If so, does the time-to-reward payoff mean it's worth focussing on a 'small' problem or two first? That buys you time and head-space to solve the bigger things.

Let Small Bad Things Happen

As you get more successful, you will always end up with more problems than you (and/or your team) can deal with. And these are the 10% that should be ignored.

If a problem isn't going to have a major impact, and isn't going to escalate to an ongoing mess, and isn't going to waste a minute of everyone's time every time they perform a task (the 'compound' problem), then declare it as "never going to be solved".

Allowing 'small bad things' to happen frees up a large amount of your time and energy to focus on the potentially big bad things!

Individual Problems

When looking at a problem on its own, you'll find that sometimes it's so involved, with so many factors that it can't be solved. You just can't know the answer. And this is where heuristic problem solving comes in, which we'll talk about right now...

It's another application of 80/20. If you can't solve 100% of the problem, can you solve 80% of the symptoms by tackling a simpler 20% of the whole problem?

Heuristic problem solving says, in a nutshell,

"If you can't solve the problem, come up with a simpler problem that you can solve."

Here's an idea of the process...

"Is doing X a good idea?" - I don't know.
"Will I be successful if I do X?" - I don't know.
"Are there people who are successful doing X?" - Yes.
"How do they do X?" - I don't know.
"Can I find out how they do X?" - Yes.

It's a great way to identify the smaller tasks to complete in order to learn the answer to the 'harder' problem.

The above sequence, for example, could lead you to network with a bunch of people who have done "X", possibly picking up a mentor along the way, and learning a new set of skills that will make an answer to the first question much easier to figure out.

Good Enough

The answers you come up with to your simpler problems may be enough to make the original problem redundant. You could have a "good enough" answer.

Or if the original problem is still relevant and necessary to solve, your heuristic solution will lead you along the right path to solve the whole.

The 20%...

Don't try to solve every problem. Solve the important (or quick-win) stuff and let small bad things happen.

If a problem has no solution, find a simpler problem that you can solve.

8. Simplifying Everything

> *"Perfection is achieved not when there's nothing left to add, but when there's nothing left to take away"*
> — Antoine de St. Exupery

The Trap of Pleasing People

It's so tempting, while we're busy trying to please everyone, to create new products, new payment plans, new services, new upsells, new schemes, new campaigns... the problem comes, though when you try to keep track of it all.

Many businesses end up so convoluted that it's impossible to really know what they do. They've somehow lost track of their core offering; that one single product or service that the rest of the business is built around.

The Big Menu

If you've ever looked at a large restaurant menu, you'll know exactly what I'm talking about.

The restuarant with sixty dishes available almost always struggles. In fact, the customers at such a restaurant almost always struggle... they're overwhelmed by choices and can't pick one. And when they do pick one, they know it won't be executed very well. How can it be? In order to provide such a large menu, it all has to be frozen and microwaved.

The restaurant with five choices normally does much better. They charge more. They have happier customers. The chef has an easier life. They have the time and energy to uphold high standards. They use fresh food.

Your "Menu"

When you look at your "menu"—your full list of products and/or services—which of them truly serve your goals? Which are in tune with your core business values? Which of them bring value to the world? Which of them are merely good and which are great?

If you dropped 50% of your products today, how many of the great products would you need to sell to make up the difference? Most likely not double.

If you dropped 90% of your products today and really focussed on shouting about your core range, would your message be stronger? Would you attract more of the right sort of clients?

Which products/services take up most of your time? Which ones are most rewarding; for you? for your clients? for your life fulfillment? for your finances?

What does your price list look like? Is it a complicated mish-mash of numbers, or can you see what's going on at a glance?

Marketing

It's the same with marketing. How many campaigns do you have running right now? Are they tested, measured and optimal, or are you winging it somewhat?

Should you spend time tracking ten different marketing campaigns, or have just one that you're keeping a close watch over?

Before you launch another campaign, look at what you already have running. Is it working? Could it work better? Should it be dropped?

It's better to have one campaign that's running really well than having ten campaigns that are not being tested, measured and improved.

Once one campaign is running smoothly by all means park it, leave it running and focus on a new one. But note it will need re-visiting again in the future.

The Spring Clean

It's worth having a look at your business occasionally and giving it a 'spring clean'. I have a three-pass method I use for most 'spring cleaning' tasks...

1. Discard Rubbish

Go through and discard the obvious "rubbish". This is the stuff that will just get in the way when you're trying to make decisions later. But if there's any doubt, keep it.

2. Archive

Go through again and archive the stuff that you're pretty sure you won't need, but might just be relevant in the future.

3. Sort

Now go through what's left and take action on it. File stuff, simplify stuff, improve stuff, do stuff.

80/20 to 50/1

The 80/20 law says—when taken a step or two further—that it's likely that 50% of your income comes from 1% of your product line. For many businesses, that means there's one core product that accounts for half of your income, and if improved could replace the income of the other 99%.

Read that again. There's a chance you can make *exactly the same income* by doubling the best 1% of your product/service line *and discarding the rest.*

It depends, naturally, on market saturation and other factors, so you'll have to check your own numbers. But you'll be surprised how often most business are pretty close to this rule.

Could you do away with all the pain, the admin overhead and the confusion of you and your clients by significantly simplifying your offering?

Always worth considering.

The 20%...

What's causing you to feel overwhelmed? What overheads are dragging you down?

How much of your business and life could you pare back?

How much growth would the effective bits need in order to replace the less effective bits?

9. Shooting for the High End

> *"Do you keep pace with those around you, or do you decide yourself just how you will live your life? The truth is... only you are qualified to set your standards. Only you can determine how you should live and what you will finally expect from yourself."*
> — Steve Goodier

On Hamburgers

Let's look at the most expensive hamburger in the world. When you hear how much it costs, you'll think "how stupid!" You'll wonder why anyone in their right mind would pay that much for a hamburger. But there's a very important lesson to be learnt. So read on...

Your basic hamburger from your basic fast-food franchise costs 99p. Naturally they don't make any money on that, but they do make money on everything they sell with the hamburger. Especially if you go large, as they are invariably trained to suggest.

Your decent hamburger from a decent hamburger place costs, what? Six quid? Maybe a tenner. Even sixteen or twenty for a really nice gourmet one from a gourmet place.

The $5,000 Burger

The world's most expensive hamburger (at the time of writing) is Las Vegas Chef Hubert Keller's *FleurBurger 5000*. Containing Wagyu beef, truffle, foie gras and other premium ingredients, a FleurBurger will set you back $5,000. Plus the service charge, naturally.

So... as I said... ridiculous! But what's the lesson?

The Money Is Out There

The lesson is that someone out there has the money for anything you can throw at them.
If you think there's a scarcity of money in the world, you've got it all wrong... there's an absolute abundance, and 80/20 helps you to tap into where that money is.

Now, you might not want to produce a Fleur-Burger (or its equivalent in your industry), but it's helpful to know that if you did produce one, there would be a market for it somewhere.

Bring It Down To Earth

Bring it down to a $500 burger, and you've increased your market massively, and are still making an extremely handsome profit.

Bring it down to a $50 burger, which is still pretty expensive, and you're now in a market that you can reach easily, if you do it right.

The maths says that if you have, for instance, 100 people all willing to pay £5 for a burger, then there are 10 of those people who were willing to pay £35 if only you had the right burger to offer them (or burger-making machine).

What's more, the top dog in your list had £264 to splash out today. It's an eye-opener.

Marketing to the Affluent

The key phrase in this chapter is *"if only you had the right X to offer them"* and this is where the work begins.

(But don't for a minute think of hard slog, this is fun and joyous and imagniative work we're going to be doing!)

The rule of 80/20 only says that people have the money to spend on your high-end product, not that they'd *want* the product you're offering. For them to want it, you'll need to really think about what's important to your potential clients.

The Values of the Affluent

High-end, big-spending clients have a totally different set of needs to Joe or Jane Public. They don't tend to care how much actual money they give up for the thing they get; but they can be very picky on the quality of the thing. And often more so on how they're treated in the delivery of the thing.

Marketing to the affluent is a whole area of study that I won't go into in this book, because it has already been more than covered by writers such as Dan Kennedy. If you'd like to learn more check out his book *"No B.S. Marketing to the Affluent: The No Holds Barred, Kick Butt, Take No Prisoners Guide to Getting Really Rich"*

The Best In The World

If you're truly interested in marketing to wealthy clients (and I can recommend it for the positive effect it has on your mood as well as your bank balance), then you're going to have to start thinking about how you'd operate if you were the best in the world at what you do.

It's a simple thought exercise, but it does require an investment of time. Actually sit down for a couple of hours with a blank sheet of paper and write down how you would operate your business if it was the best in the world.

What would you offer? How would you answer the phone? What would your literature look like? What words would you use? What words *wouldn't* you use? What would you wear?

Once you have the 'ideal' business on paper, apply the 80/20 principle. Don't try to fix everything in one go, but have a look at the most effective things you can begin implementing today to move your business towards being the best.

Standards

Roger Hamilton has a fantastic analogy for standards in his book, *"The Millionaire Master Plan"*... He says that your standards are the platform you stand on. If you're trying to reach a light-bulb on a high ceiling, the higher the platform you stand on the less you'll have to stretch.

It's just the same with your goals... to reach your lofty goals, set high standards and live to them.

So next time you're having a "blue sky" day, have a think about the highest-end product or service you could offer. And if anyone ever actually buys it, come up with a new one at a whole new level above that one!

The 20%...

The money is out there for anything you want to offer.

But recognise that you'll be on a different playing field and must play appropriately to the new set of standards and rules.

10. Talking to Busy People

> *"When someone tells you they are too 'busy'... It's not a reflection of their schedule; it's a reflection of YOUR spot on their schedule."*
> — Steve Maraboli

Make it Easy

Most people—if they haven't read this book and implemented 80/20 in their life—are busy. They're scrabbling for time. They don't want to waste time reading the stuff you send to them, whether that's an offer, a quote, an invoice or anything else.

The plain and simple truth is that they're not willing to prioritise you on their schedule.

So make it easy for them, and the quickest way you can make things easy is through a "dual readership path".

A whatty what?

A "dual readership path". It's the 80/20 way of writing. You convey 80% of the meaning of your communication in 20% of the writing, and make it easy to spot.

Dual Readership Path

There are a number of ways to create a dual-readership path. The most popular are:

- Key Facts Sheet
- Summary Boxes
- Images with Captions
- Selective Bold Paragraphs
- Bullet Lists
- Subheadings

When you present a slab of grey text (which is what a plain page of text looks like), the 'lazy' brain doesn't bother reading.

All of the dual readership path methods allow the reader to pick through quickly for what interests them, and then get more detail where needed.

Utility Bills

Have a look at a utility bill right now. I bet you the price, how to pay and the company's contact number are really easy to pick out at a glance.

They've chosen the things people will be most interested in and made them stand out.

If you want to find out exactly how many kilowatt hours you used this month, it'll be there somewhere, but you'll have to search for it.

It's Your Responsibility to be Understood

You can do the same with your correspondance.

Make it easy for your readers to get the key points that you'd like to convey, then fill in the details around them where necessary.

The moment you accept responsibility for your readers' being busy (or lazy) you will find your communications immediately being much more widely read, and having a greater response rate.

You'll notice, for example, that this book offers sub-headings that are easy to pick out; and also the all-important *"The 20%..."* sections summarising the chapter, so if you revisit the book, you won't have to read the whole of each chapter again.

These little details just make the task of reading simpler, and could boost your response rates massively. Give it a go!

And you're probably busy, so I'll end the chapter there(!)

The 20%...

People are busy (and lazy).

Make it easy for them to read what you're sending to them and they're more likely to read and respond.

The Common Thread

> *"Doing less is not being lazy. Don't give in to a culture that values personal sacrifice over personal productivity."*
> — *Tim Ferriss*

Start Living 80/20

So you've read your two chapters, and it's a good bet that 20% of you will have implemented everything you need to in order to seriously transform your business and your life.

(And, naturally 20% will do nothing and the middle 60% will do *some* of it.)

Now are you ready to start *really* living 80/20?

The Simple Steps

Read the other chapters by all means, but you'll spot the common thread running through all of them, and this is it, in the most simple steps...

1. Pick something that needs fixing.
2. Sort according to a smart measurement.
3. Sack off the bottom 10% as worthy of ignoring.
4. Pick the top 20% that will have most impact.
5. Invest time and energy into that 20%.
6. Return to step 1.

80/20 Is Everywhere

You'll be amazed—once you start living 80/20—how often it shows up in life (basically everywhere!)

It can take time, though, to really start *seeing* properly. To spot the opportunities to use the 80/20 principle to simplify your life and business, and improve your effectiveness.

80/20 On Steroids

A common misconception with the 80/20 rule is that people think the 80 and the 20 are on the same scale, and therefore must add up to 100.

It's worth noting, though, that they're on *different* scales. The 20 is measuring *effort*, while the 80 is measuring *results*.

This difference in scales is even more apparant than when 80/20 is applied to itself; in that top 20% of efforts lies *another* 80/20. So 20% of the top 20% of actions lead to 80% of the top 80% of the results...

Don't worry about the maths right now, suffice to say the result is that 4% of actions lead to about 64% of results.

And by splitting the top of the 64/4 results with another 80/20 we reach the extreme conclusion that, 1% of actions lead to around 50% of results.

Just pause for a moment and think about the implications of that sentence.

You could achieve half *of your current results for just* one percent *of your current effort.*

100% Results For 2% Effort

Taken another step further, by doubling the most highly effective stuff you have to offer, you could end up with 100% of results you previously achieved. For just 2% of the original effort. This is where the real gold of 80/20 lies.

Naturally it doesn't always work exactly like this, but to live 80/20 is to constantly focus on what is working best and capitalise on it.

Mindset

Mindset issues can raise their ugly head when working with 80/20 to the extreme. Have a look again at Tim Ferriss' quote at the top of this chapter – and read his book *The Four Hour Work*

Week for many examples of 80/20 taken to extreme ends.

Our culture puts such an emphasis on trying hard. It pushes home the message that if you're not *busy* then you are not *valuable*.

According to the bulk of the working population it is somehow a *virtue* to work inefficiently and burn yourself out while presenting less than your best value to the world. As long as you're busy.

It's crazy when you stop to think about it.

The 'Struggle' Blueprint

If you believe that struggle is a virtue, please read T. Harv Ecker's *"Secrets of The Millionaire Mind"*. As mentioned in section 2, it deals very much with the blueprint we pick up from our genetics, our parents, our peers and our teachers.

These are the people who have, throughout our lives, tried to stop us going out there; to keep us safe, to prevent us from taking the risks that could lead to success. They could, naturally lead to failure too, but you'll never find out if you don't take them!

These people often can't even *imagine* the goals we're setting for ourselves, let alone imagine that we would succeed at them.

In Conclusion

Success with 80/20 comes from habitual and disciplined application of knowledge, awareness, mindset, smart analysis and most importantly *action*.

Good luck!

Resources

If you like what you've read here and you'd like to take your 80/20 journey further, there are resources available on my website:

http://www.stuartcarter.co.uk/8020book

Good luck, and do let me know how you get along. You can email, or connect on facebook or twitter...

Email: 8020book@stuartcarter.co.uk
Facebook: www.facebook.com/stuartcarteruk
Twitter: @stuartcarteruk

Stay in touch,

Stuart Carter

Further Reading

General Principles

"The 80/20 Principle: The Secret to Achieving More with Less"
Richard Koch *(ISBN: 978-0385491747)*

Chapter 2

"Secrets of The Millionaire Mind"
T. Harv Ecker *(ISBN: 978-0749927899)*

"The Big Leap: Conquer Your Hidden Fear and Take Life to the Next Level"
Gay Hendricks *(ISBN: 978-0061735363)*

Chapter 3

"80/20 Sales and Marketing: The Definitive Guide to Working Less and Making More"
Perry Marshall *(ISBN: 978-1599185057)*

Chapter 4

"The Big Leap: Conquer Your Hidden Fear and Take Life to the Next Level"
Gay Hendricks *(ISBN: 978-0061735363)*

Chapter 9

"No B.S. Marketing to the Affluent: The No Holds Barred, Kick Butt, Take No Prisoners Guide to Getting Really Rich"
Dan S. Kennedy *(ISBN: 978-1599181813)*

"The Millionaire Master Plan: Your Personalized Path To Financial Success"
Roger James Hamilton *(ISBN: 978-1455549238)*

The Common Thread

"The Four Hour Work Week"
Tim Ferriss *(ISBN: 978-0091929114)*

About the Author

Stuart Carter is an award-winning business owner, coach, Master Mind facilitator and speaker.

He started a photography business in 2009 after redundancy from a soulless computer programming job, and spent the year 2013-14 in a conscious growth effort applying the 80/20 principle wherever he could.

The results surprised him when he doubled his revenue and halved his working hours.

He realised that he loved business—and particularly 80/20—more than photography and went on a mission to share what he had learnt about business, productivity and the magic of 80/20 with other ambitious business owners like you!

NOTES

Made in the USA
Charleston, SC
23 September 2015